The Scientific Method
IN ACTION

ANSWER!
ANALYZE YOUR DATA

Emma Carlson Berne

PowerKiDS press

New York

Published in 2015 by The Rosen Publishing Group, Inc.
29 East 21st Street, New York, NY 10010

First Edition

Editor: Jennifer Way
Book Design: Kate Vlachos
Photo Research: Katie Stryker

Photo Credits: Cover JGI/Tom Grill/Blend Images/Getty Images; pp. 5, 12 Fuse/Thinkstock; p. 6 Lucidio Studio, Inc./Flickr/Getty Images; pp. 7, 14 Purestock/Thinkstock; pp. 8, 11, 18, 19, 21 iStockphoto/Thinkstock; p. 9 Image Source/Getty Images; p. 10 Jupiterimages/Brand X Pictures/ Thinkstock; p. 13 Klaus Vedfelt/Riser/Getty Images; p. 15 Compassionate Eye Foundation/ Robert Daly/OJO Images/Riser/Getty Images; p. 16 Katrina Wittkamp/Digital Vision/Getty Images; p. 20 Chris Wahlberg/Workbook Stock/Getty Images; p. 22 Photos.com/Thinkstock.

Library of Congress Cataloging-in-Publication Data

Berne, Emma Carlson, author.
 Answer! : analyze your data / by Emma Carlson Berne. — First edition.
    pages cm. — (The scientific method in action)
 Includes index.
 ISBN 978-1-4777-2930-4 (library) — ISBN 978-1-4777-3017-1 (pbk.) —
 ISBN 978-1-4777-3088-1 (6-pack)
 1. Science–Methodology—Juvenile literature. 2. Research—Juvenile literature.
 3. Science—Experiments—Juvenile literature. I. Title.
 Q175.2.B47 2015
 507.2'1—dc23
                              2013027104

Manufactured in the United States of America

CPSIA Compliance Information: Batch #WS14PK5: For Further Information contact Rosen Publishing, New York, New York at 1-800-237-9932

CONTENTS

Exploring the Scientific Method 4

Collecting Data 6

A Variety of Data 8

Analyzing Data 10

Summarize Your Results 12

Using Graphic Organizers 14

Making Connections 17

Proving or Disproving Your Hypothesis 18

Making Revisions.......................................20

Great Discoveries......................................22

Glossary..23

Index 24

Websites 24

EXPLORING THE SCIENTIFIC METHOD

There are six steps that make up the **scientific method**. First, you make **observations** and ask questions. Next, you form a **hypothesis**, and then plan an **experiment**. The experiment gives you information to collect. Next comes **analyzing** the results. Finally, you share your results.

The scientific method is a plan that scientists use to ask and answer questions about the world. To investigate these questions, scientists design and perform experiments. Then they look at the results of their experiment carefully. This is called analyzing **data**. You will learn more about this step in the scientific method in the chapters that follow.

Running an experiment is just one part of a scientific investigation. Learning how to analyze your data allows you to determine the meaning in your results.

5

No matter what kind of experiment you conduct, you need to repeat it several times under the same conditions.

When scientists conduct experiments, they collect data. They take notes on what happens to the **control** and to the **variables** in their experiments and then write up their observations.

For example, you might design an experiment to see if a small, heavy object will hit the ground faster than a larger, lighter object when dropped from a certain height. Your hypothesis is that the heavier object will hit the ground first. You then perform your experiment many times and note the results each time. All of these results are your data. Next, you will examine your data to see if your hypothesis was correct.

The data you collect could be different kinds of information, such as temperature, length, or time.

A VARIETY OF DATA

Taking photographs lets you create a record of the changes you see in an experiment.

You will collect different kinds of data when you run your experiment. The kind of data will depend on the kind of experiment you performed.

You might have a page of observation notes. Did you take photographs or a video of your experiment? This is data, too.

Perhaps you used a tape measure, a timer, or a thermometer to measure changes. You would then have a list of measurements and times. Perhaps some of your friends took part in your experiment. Did they fill out surveys or write notes of their own? You might even have a chart or a graph you drew up.

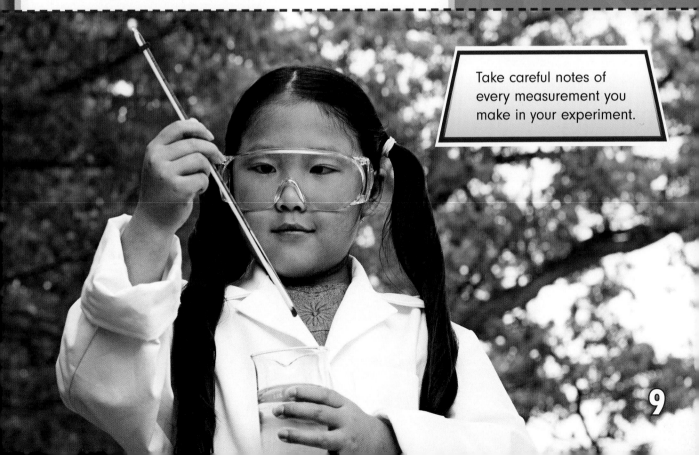

Take careful notes of every measurement you make in your experiment.

Analyzing data means carefully going over your experiment results, with the goal of finding out if the results support your hypothesis or disprove it. When scientists analyze their data, they are able to figure out what it means.

You might use a computer to calculate and to write up your notes.

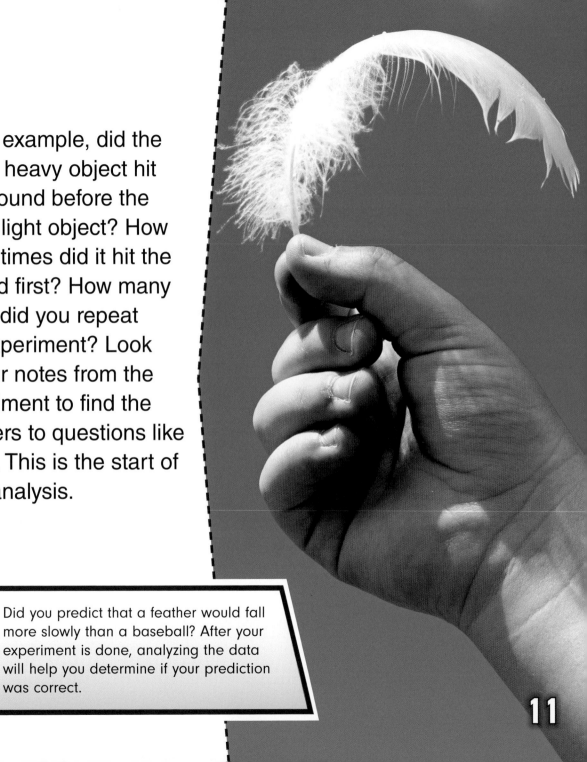

For example, did the small, heavy object hit the ground before the large, light object? How many times did it hit the ground first? How many times did you repeat the experiment? Look at your notes from the experiment to find the answers to questions like these. This is the start of your analysis.

Did you predict that a feather would fall more slowly than a baseball? After your experiment is done, analyzing the data will help you determine if your prediction was correct.

SUMMARIZE YOUR RESULTS

You might have a lot of data to look over. **Summarizing** can help you explain all of your results in a way that you and others can easily understand.

To summarize, neatly copy down the key results from the raw data of

You should write up how many times you dropped each ball in your summary. You should also note from what height you dropped each ball and how long it took each ball to hit the ground.

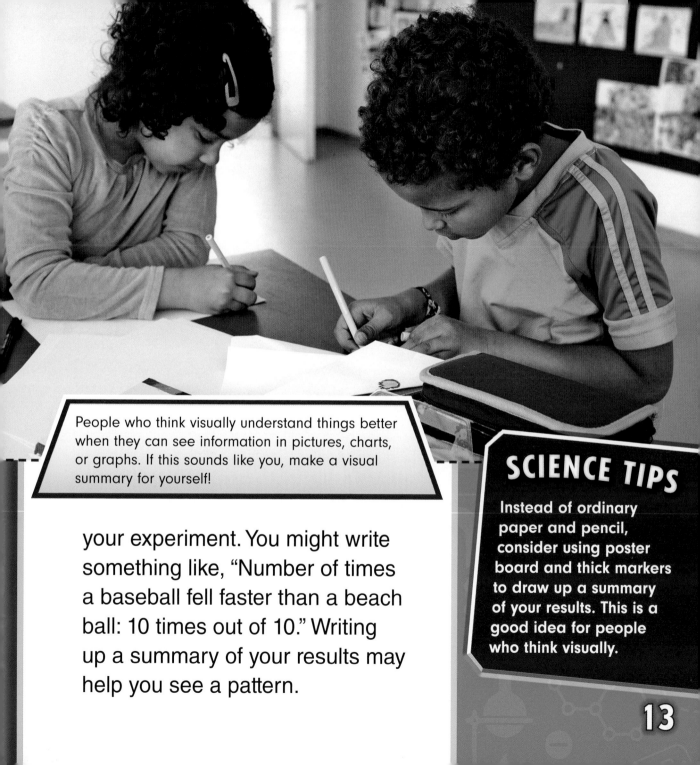

People who think visually understand things better when they can see information in pictures, charts, or graphs. If this sounds like you, make a visual summary for yourself!

SCIENCE TIPS

Instead of ordinary paper and pencil, consider using poster board and thick markers to draw up a summary of your results. This is a good idea for people who think visually.

your experiment. You might write something like, "Number of times a baseball fell faster than a beach ball: 10 times out of 10." Writing up a summary of your results may help you see a pattern.

USING GRAPHIC ORGANIZERS

Using a computer program, you can input measurements from your results and it will create a chart or graph for you.

To help identify patterns, it is a good idea to show your results as a graphic organizer, such as a chart or a graph. Bar graphs are best for displaying the differences in measurements, amounts, or temperatures. Pie charts are best for showing percentages. Line graphs are best at displaying the differences that have occurred over time.

You can always carefully measure and draw graphic organizers by hand. However, computer-drawn graphic organizers are more accurate and easier to read than hand-drawn ones. Ask your teacher or librarian to show you a program for making graphs or charts.

These kids are looking at a bar graph on their tablet computers.

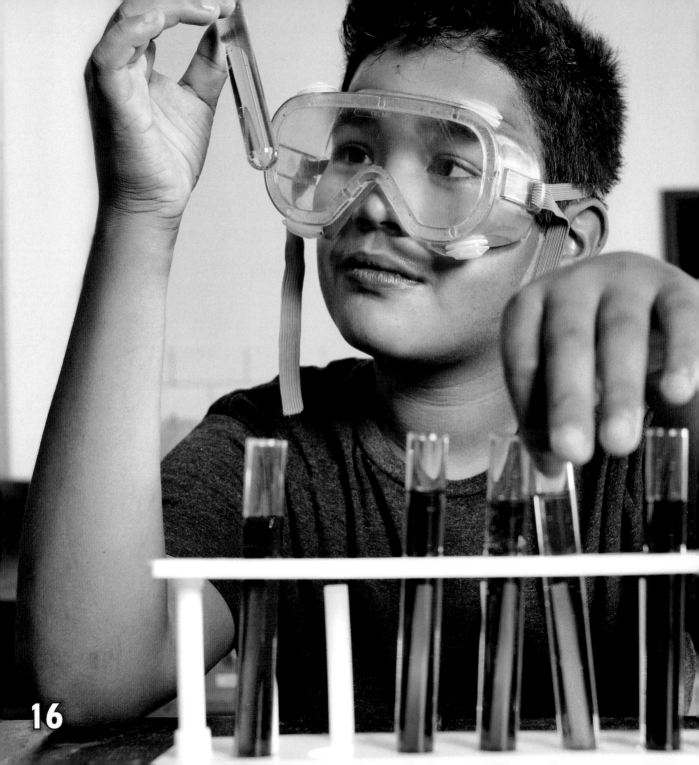

MAKING CONNECTIONS

You have collected your data, summarized it, and created graphic organizers. Now it is time to focus on the patterns that you can see emerging to further analyze your results. Your charts should help you with that.

For example, when analyzing your data, can you see if the large, light object always hit the ground before the small, heavy object? How many times out of how many times? Can you make a connection between the weight of the object, the size of the object, and the rate at which it fell? Making these connections in your analysis will help you draw your **conclusions**.

When you analyze your data, you are making connections among the things you observed during your experiment.

PROVING OR DISPROVING YOUR HYPOTHESIS

Now you are at the moment of the scientific process in which you will conclude whether your hypothesis has been proven or disproven. For example, say your hypothesis was that a beach ball will fall more slowly than a baseball when dropped from a height of 6 feet.

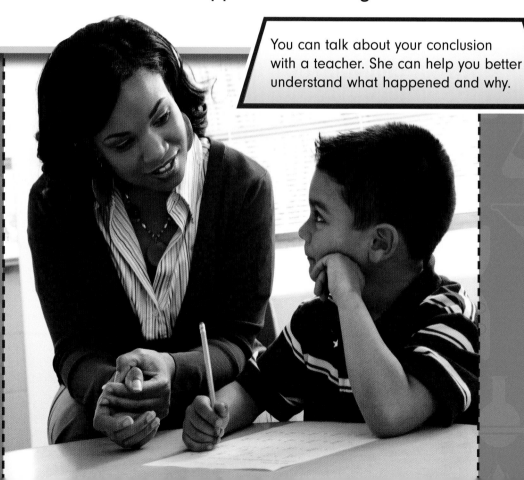

You can talk about your conclusion with a teacher. She can help you better understand what happened and why.

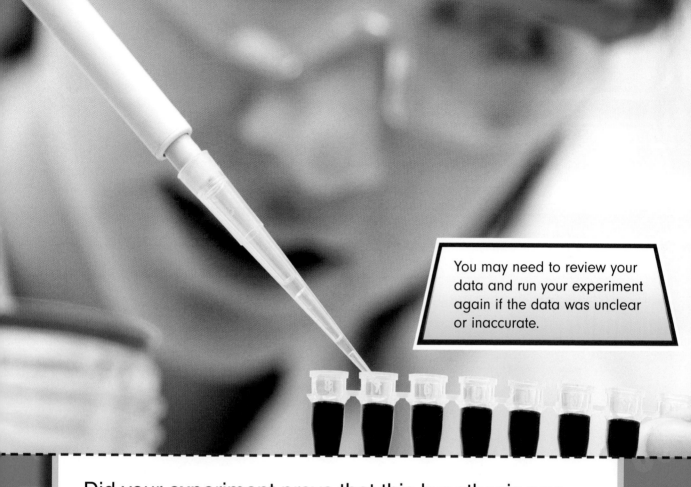

You may need to review your data and run your experiment again if the data was unclear or inaccurate.

Did your experiment prove that this hypothesis was true? If so, then you have successfully proven your hypothesis.

Do not worry if your hypothesis was disproven, though. This happens to scientists all the time. Look at your data again. Does it point to why your hypothesis was wrong? Understanding your conclusion is more important than having a correct hypothesis.

MAKING REVISIONS

Scientists, such as astronomers, revise their hypotheses and make new observations when their first hypothesis turns out to be wrong.

Perhaps your hypothesis was indeed incorrect. Adult scientists develop wrong hypotheses all the time. In fact, a wrong hypothesis is an opportunity to develop a new experiment.

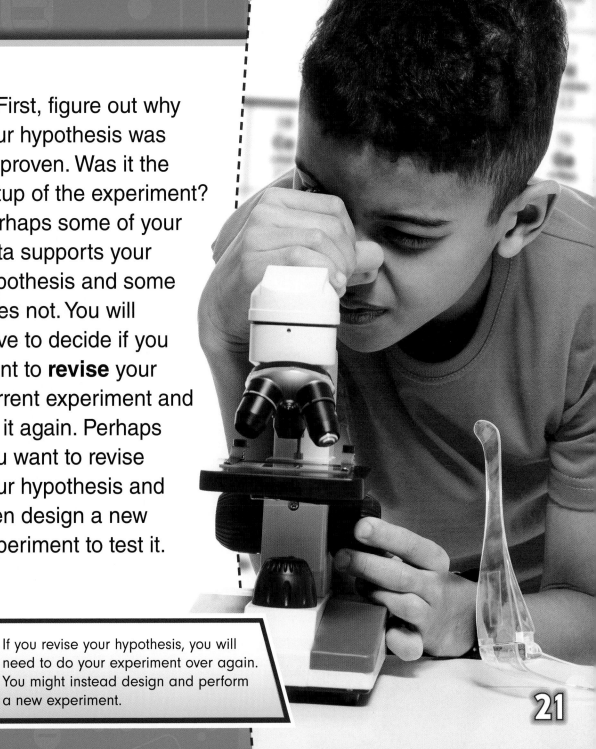

First, figure out why your hypothesis was disproven. Was it the setup of the experiment? Perhaps some of your data supports your hypothesis and some does not. You will have to decide if you want to **revise** your current experiment and do it again. Perhaps you want to revise your hypothesis and then design a new experiment to test it.

If you revise your hypothesis, you will need to do your experiment over again. You might instead design and perform a new experiment.

Running an experiment, analyzing the results, and drawing conclusions are important steps in making scientific discoveries. In the late 1800s, Marie Curie studied **radiation**. She hypothesized that there was an element no one had discovered that was giving off a very strong radiation.

Curie performed many experiments and analyzed her data carefully. She found that there were actually two new radioactive elements no one knew existed. She was awarded the **Nobel Prize** for her discoveries.

Marie Curie discovered the elements radium and polonium.

GLOSSARY

analyzing (A-nuh-lyz-ing) Examining something carefully and thinking about what it means.

conclusions (kun-KLOO-zhunz) The judgments that can be made after studying results.

control (kun-TROHL) The standard of an experiment that produces what is expected for a result.

data (DAY-tuh) Facts.

experiment (ik-SPER-uh-ment) A test done on something to learn more about it.

hypothesis (hy-PAH-theh-ses) Something that is suggested to be true for the purpose of an experiment or argument.

Nobel Prize (noh-BEL PRYZ) An award of money given each year to a person or a group for work in a subject, such as literature.

observations (ahb-ser-VAY-shunz) Things that are seen or noticed.

radiation (ray-dee-AY-shun) Rays of light, heat, or energy that spread outward from something.

revise (rih-VYZ) To make changes to or improvements in something.

scientific method (sy-en-TIH-fik MEH-thud) The system of running experiments in science.

summarizing (SUH-muh-ryz-ing) Making a short account of something that has been said or written.

variables (VER-ee-uh-bulz) Elements in an experiment that may be changed.

23

INDEX

C
conclusion(s), 17, 19, 22

E
experiment(s), 4, 6–11, 13, 19–22

H
hypothesis, 4, 7, 10, 18–21

L
list, 9

M
measurements, 9, 14

N
Nobel Prize, 22
notes, 6, 8–9, 11

O
object, 6–7, 11, 17
observations, 4, 6

P
plan, 4

Q
questions, 4, 11

R
results, 4, 7, 10, 12–14, 17, 22

S
step(s), 4, 22
surveys, 9

V
variables, 6
video, 8

WEBSITES

Due to the changing nature of Internet links, PowerKids Press has developed an online list of websites related to the subject of this book. This site is updated regularly. Please use this link to access the list:
www.powerkidslinks.com/smia/data/